Mickey the Monarch

Based on a True Story

by

Audrey Sommers

illustrated by

Julia Bhuiyan

HMSI
Publishing L.L.C.

Mickey the Monarch

Published by HMSI Publishing
www.PublishHMSI.com

By
Audrey Sommers

Illustrated By
Julia Bhuiyan

Editing by
Monica Tombers
Mattie Dugan

Design by
Ilya

Cover Design by
Julia Bhuiyan

Publishing Coordination by
Jessica A. Paredes

Published by
David R. Haslam

Permissions,
HMSI Publishing,
2209 Pinecroft Dr.,
Canton, MI 48188, U.S.A.

info@PublishHMSI.com
Tel.: 734-259-0387

ISBN – 13: 978-0-9851996-2-3

0082-0001

Printed in the United States of America

TKR 10 9 8 7 6 5 4 3 2 1
MK 31527-23898
ILYA-V 41546 15:59 PT

To all the creatures in nature

The animal kingdom is a wondrous place, full of creatures who can amaze us with their beauty and behavior. If you watch nature carefully, you will discover all sorts of interesting stories for yourself. Here is a story of caring and compassion between two unlikely friends...

Mickey was born to fly. He dreamed of flying to far off lands.

You see, Mickey was a magnificent monarch butterfly, and all monarchs are born to fly! Some, like Mickey, get to take an amazing journey that fills young butterflies' dreams.

Each year, as the leaves begin turning the colors of their wings, these monarchs gather by the thousands at Point Pelee National Park in Canada to begin their southerly trek. They fly across Lake Erie, over the continental United States and down to Mexico to escape the cold northern winter. There, they live in the warm sunshine until the next spring. When their wings start to itch, they begin their 2,000 mile journey home.

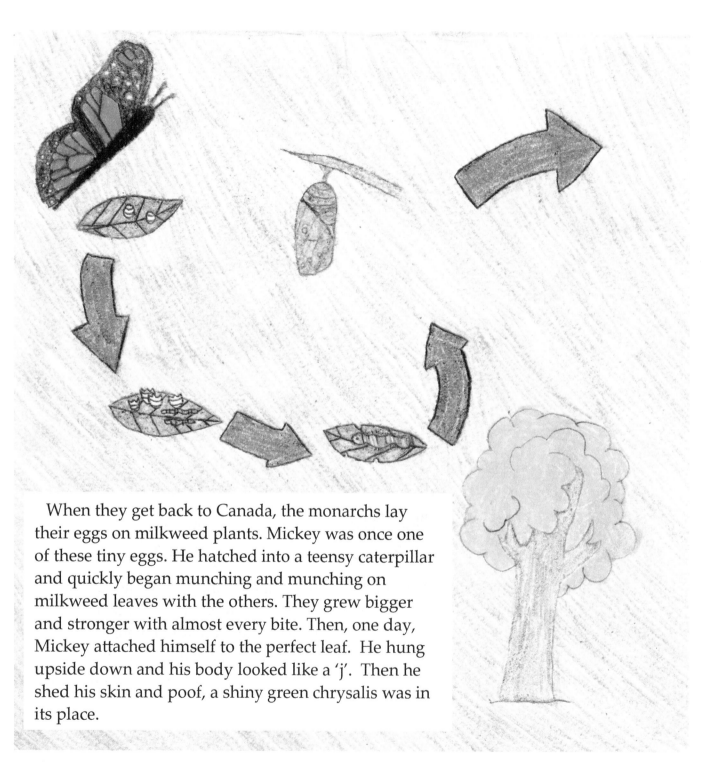

When they get back to Canada, the monarchs lay their eggs on milkweed plants. Mickey was once one of these tiny eggs. He hatched into a teensy caterpillar and quickly began munching and munching on milkweed leaves with the others. They grew bigger and stronger with almost every bite. Then, one day, Mickey attached himself to the perfect leaf. He hung upside down and his body looked like a 'j'. Then he shed his skin and poof, a shiny green chrysalis was in its place.

After about two weeks, the chrysalis broke open and Mickey the Monarch emerged. Mickey was part of the third generation of monarchs born this year, the generation that would make the trip to Mexico for the winter.

Little Mickey came out of his chrysalis in mid-September and unfolded his colorful wings to dry. He'd worked very hard in that chrysalis, and he was proud to finally call himself a butterfly.

Soon, he was flying way up to the tops of the hackberry trees and then down near the ground to drink the delicious nectar of the wildflowers.

Being an insect, Mickey couldn't know about his impressive heritage. Born in the early summer, the previous generations of monarch butterflies were destined to live only a few weeks. Migratory Monarchs, like Mickey, were born in the late summer, somehow knowing that the time to follow the warmth was coming.

No, Mickey couldn't understand genes, the things that made his body different and more durable than the monarchs born before him. He only cared about flowers and flying. Fluttering fast through the park's woods and grasslands was what he loved to do best.

Late Setember came, with tons of brightly colored leaves swirling in the chilly wind. It was finally time to migrate, but something had happened to poor Mickey's wings! Maybe the wind had blown him into a tree, or a big drop of rain had hit him. His wings weren't doing their job, and flying was harder than usual.

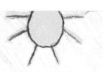

The other monarchs prepared for their nearly 2,000 mile journey. Mickey found himself lying alone on the shore of Lake Erie as the others took off, with only stones and weathered pieces of wood to keep him company.

A strong wind blew across the water. It was getting cold and Mickey couldn't help but shiver. Using the little energy he had left, he took flight one more time.

Mickey didn't know what to do. There were no flowers nor friends nor hackberry trees as he flew over the seemingly endless water. He began to cry as he struggled in the cool air. After several hours, Mickey landed in a place he'd never been…a neighborhood.

Later that day, an eight-year-old boy was walking home from school with his dad.

"Dad, look at this! A butterfly just lying here on the path!" he exclaimed. "His wings are moving, but it looks like he's hurt. He can't fly. Can I take him home, Dad?"

The boy's dad sadly shook his head and said, "No, Aiden. He is part of nature. We should leave him."

But Aiden persisted. "Please, Dad! He will die here if we don't do something!"

So, Aiden's dad agreed and gently lifted Mickey into his hands. "I have an old shoebox in my closet," he said. "We'll make him comfortable. After all, this butterfly may live only a night or two at best."

Mickey spent that first night in the open shoebox near Aiden's bed. He felt relieved to be someplace warmer and safer. Mickey settled in and fell asleep.

The next day, before he left for school, Aiden carried the injured butterfly to the flower garden in the backyard to frolic until he returned home. He hoped the little creature would be safe for the day.

When Aiden came home from school, he raced to the garden to see if the butterfly was still there.

Sure enough, the monarch was waiting for him on a flower.

"I'm home!" Aiden told his new friend. "I've been wondering all day what I should call you, but none of the names I think of seem right."

The butterfly fluttered his wings and circled Aiden's head. As the butterfly drifted past his ears, Aiden thought he heard a faint noise that sounded like the word "Mickey." "Mickey?" Aiden repeated aloud. Aiden's arm tickled a bit as the monarch landed lightly on him. "Mickey it is!" Aiden said, smiling.

Aiden wanted a proper home for Mickey. So, with Dad's help, he made the shoebox into a tiny apartment. They put the shoebox in the small bathroom, the warmest room in the house. Mom bought a small bouquet of flowers and put them in the box. Now Mickey could eat and rest in the warmth.

"I love you, Mickey," Aiden said. He gently put Mickey to bed on a flower in his small bathroom apartment. "Good night," Aiden whispered as he turned out the light, leaving the soft glow of the nightlight to keep his butterfly friend company.

"How could someone love me so much when I look like this, with my broken wings?" Mickey thought to himself when Aiden said goodnight. "Why does this boy take such good care of me when I can't give him anything in return?" the butterfly wondered.

Over the next few weeks, Mickey grew weaker. He often sat motionless on a flower, sometimes for hours. Mickey wondered how he could make the boy understand that these flowers weren't providing him with the food he desperately needed. Aiden knew something was wrong, but he was having trouble figuring it out.

However, Aiden knew he had to do something. He realized the nectar from fresh flowers kept Mickey alive, but what else could he give him after the flowers had dried up? It had become clear that there was no nectar for his dear monarch to drink.

Aiden asked Mom and Dad to help
him with the ailing butterfly. When he
looked it up on the internet, Dad learned
that butterflies need to drink sugar from a natural source,
like nectar, fruit or honey.

With Mom's help, Aiden cut up a pear and prepared a
liquid mixture of honey and water for Mickey.

When Aiden entered Mickey's bathroom, the monarch immediately smelled the sweetness, put out his proboscis, and drank the pear juice. Then he moved to the spoon Aiden was holding out. It was full of sweet honey-water. The monarch drank slowly. It was nearly ten minutes by the time he was full. After, Mickey fell fast asleep under a flower. Aiden knew he had done the right thing.

That night, Dad told Aiden, "You know, Mickey isn't a pet like a dog or a cat. Mickey is a butterfly who won't live long. He is going to die soon."

"I know, Dad. But I want to give Mickey the best time possible while he is alive," Aiden replied. "Isn't Mickey like Grandpa in the nursing home? You told me Grandpa is not going to live much longer. Aren't we supposed to take care of Grandpa and other living things that are sick?" Dad thought about this for a moment, then smiled at his son. "Yes, Aiden," said Dad, realizing how the butterfly and his own father's life were so alike. "I am very proud of you, son."

The honey mixture helped keep Mickey going for another month. Aiden fed Mickey every morning before school and again after dinner.

Mickey and Aiden grew to love and know each other even more. Aiden would let Mickey sit on his hand while he did homework. The pair would even watch TV while Mickey drank from the spoon in Aiden's hand.

"I really love resting on his warm hand!" Mickey thought. Aiden happened to like it, too.

Then, one Sunday morning as the family returned from brunch, Aiden rushed to Mickey's shoebox, eager to see his friend. But something was wrong.

"Mom! Dad! Mickey isn't moving! I think he's dead!" Aiden began to cry as Dad rushed to his side.

Dad said, "Son, you gave Mickey some wonderful last weeks by taking care of him so well and giving him the love he needed. Be proud of yourself, because Mickey knows what you did."

Aiden looked lovingly at the monarch in his little bathroom apartment for the last time, thinking of how and where he could bury the tiny creature.

All of a sudden, Mickey's torn
little wings began to flutter.
    Aiden cried out in excitement,
"Mickey isn't dead, Dad! He
was only sleeping!"
    Yes, the dear butterfly was
still alive!

"I love you, Mickey, and I always will," Aiden said. "I'll do whatever I can to make you happy."

And so, Mickey the Monarch lived much longer than anyone expected, all because of a special gift: the gift of love.

Monarch Resources and References

A QR link has been included. HMSI Publishing and the author are not responsible for the maintenance or content of any external link.

Point Pelee National Park - main page
http://www.pc.gc.ca/eng/pn-np/on/pelee/index.aspx

Point Pelee National Park - Monarchs
http://www.pc.gc.ca/eng/pn-np/on/pelee/natcul/natcul5.aspx

Monarch Watch
http://www.monarchwatch.org/

Journey North/South
http://www.learner.org/jnorth/

Monarch Butterfly Website
http://www.monarch-butterfly.com/

Wikipedia Page
http://en.wikipedia.org/wiki/Monarch_butterfly

Monarch Butterfly USA Website
http://www.monarchbutterflyusa.com/MBUSA.htm

The Monarch Butterfly Grove at Pismo Beach
http://www.monarchbutterfly.org/

Kickstarter Backers

Kathy Longo
Michelle Fox
Virginia Holmes
Alice Yanity
Ronald T Klein
Pat Fader
William Stephen
Bill LaBoeuf
Khyati Naik
Sujit Datta
Jack Strickland
Debbie Lail
Sue Huang for Jamie, Ryan and Nicholas Leahy
Teri Ronan
Margaret Bagley
Cheryl Giacomino
Dale Petrusha, DDS
Rezaul Ashraf
and all the butterflies that spread their wings to help without being named...

Special Thanks

Debbie Lail who named Aiden after her grandson
&
Dr. Petrusha for his kind sponsorship

Acknowledgements

First I would like to thank my publisher, David, and his team who helped bring this story to life for children everywhere. Next, I'd like to thank the people at Point Pelee National Park in Ontario, Canada for their help and creativity, especially Monique Oltrop and Sarah Rupert for their encouragement. I would also like to thank all of the Kickstarter backers who had faith to donate to get the project to the stage of printing, especially Debbie Lail and Dale Petrusha, DDS. And finally, to my husband, Richard, for giving up our spare bathroom so a butterfly could have a home.

Audrey Sommers
Michigan
June 2013

I would like to express my great appreciation to my third grade teacher, Mrs. Jones, for recommending me to illustrate this book. Special thanks to my parents for support and inspiration to pursue one of my passions, art. I wish to acknowledge the publisher, David R. Haslam, for publishing this book. And last, but not least, thanks to Audrey Sommers for allowing me to illustrate such a wonderful story.

Julia Bhuiyan
Michigan
June 2013

Above: The real Mickey with Audrey.

34

About the Author & Illustrator

Author, Audrey Sommers is an Emmy Award winning TV producer and writer. She is also a former TV news anchor/reporter. Her work as a broadcast and print journalist has earned her numerous awards, including three Telly's and honors from the Society of Professional Journalists-Detroit Chapter for Best in Feature Reporting. *Mickey the Monarch* is her first book.

Julia Bhuiyan, the illustrator, is currently a fifth grade student in a suburban Detroit school district. She has many talents, art being just one of them. Julia and her family are very excited to see her illustrations printed in her first book.

Mickey the Monarch

CPSIA information can be obtained at www.ICGtesting.com
Printed in the USA
BVOW10s1115010914

364891BV00001B/2/P